# The Son of David
## A Meditation on the Agency of God

by

# Ralph Clark Chandler

Royce Castle Publishers Incorporated

Kalamazoo, Michigan

Design and Calligraphy by Marijo Carney
Lithographed in the United States

*This book is dedicated to my first-born son, Eli John Chandler, whose strength of character has always reminded me of the young man Jesus.*

*The calligraphy and symbols were done by my friend, Marijo Carney. This book is as much hers as it is mine.*

*Ralph Clark Chandler*
*The First Day of Advent, 1982*

# FOREWORD

*The reader will wonder about the historicity of this story. There are interpretations here which are at variance with traditional understandings of the career and personality of Jesus. The reader should bear in mind that all we know about the details of Jesus' life is what we can extrapolate from the gospels, and that they were written at least forty years after the events they purport to describe. Moreover, they were written at a time when historiography as we know it today did not exist. The gospel stories were constructed out of the message and the belief system of the early church, not the other way around.*

*The mythological material in the gospel accounts is so mixed in with historical material that modern scholars frequently cannot tell the difference. The German New Testament scholar Rudolf Bultmann was probably correct in saying that we cannot from this vantage point in history get behind the message and the belief system to "what happened" in any historical sense.*

*There are artistic and theological possibilities in that. We are free to surmise on the basis of what makes sense to us. Beyond our freedom to surmise, however, unique tools of analysis are available in the modern world. Among these are highly sophisticated linguistic analyses of Biblical texts; extra-Biblical writings, such as the works of Josephus; archaelogical evidence; psychoanalytic theory; the Dead Sea Scrolls and what they reveal about Jewish life in the intertestamental period; the results of the investigations of the Shroud of Turin; and scientific knowledge about the nature of matter and light. Each of these is a source for <u>The Son of David.</u> They make it possible to reintroduce the modern world to the man Jesus.*

This is a story about a man who decided to fulfill in his person the ancient oracles of his people about a great leader who would deliver them from bondage. The story's roots are deep in the pre-occupation of ancient Israel with the nature of God and with the idea of a messiah. Its main characters at the outset are two typical first century products of that environment: Jesus, son of Joseph and Mary of Nazareth, and John, son of Zechariah and Elizabeth of the hill country of Judah. Jesus and John are cousins. Their destinies were linked before they were born.

The young men are dreamers, but they have a practical cast of mind which includes planning for what they

want to accomplish. In their intermittent contact as they grow up, Jesus in the north, John in the south, they share the same fantasy world and eventually the same vocational goal: the restoration of prophetic leadership and the idea of the sacred in the lives of their people. Jesus is particularly influenced by the fact that he is of the house and lineage of David, his people's greatest King. He studied the career of David carefully and identified completely with the shepherd boy who, it was said became a man after God's own heart. From the Books of Samuel, Jesus knew David to be a representative man as well as a sacral King. He was a poet who lived out his poetry and danced and sang his passion for God. He was also a warrior and a statesman. Yet David lived much

of his early life as an outlaw and renegade who learned to be cunning and a manipulator of events. Like their ancestor Jacob, David wrestled with God until he gained God's blessing for what he wanted to do. His career shaped the messianic hope, for by dint of his own will David ushered in a kingdom the wise men said was God's own.

By their late teens, Jesus and John concluded that the Kingdom of David could not possibly be restored in a political sense. The idea of the Son of David, the messiah, had to be a mental and spiritual construct. The revolutionaries were wrong. The Jews could not defeat the Romans, but they could deliver themselves from the debilitations of hating them. They could re-focus. They could best do that by remembering and exploring the contemporary meaning of the only truly unique attainment in their national history: their knowledge of God.

The cousins decided to go their separate ways and prepare for their life's work. Jesus went to seek the mastery of the law, the prophets, and the wisdom literature of his people; to observe and listen to them; to learn their folk wisdom; to internalize the concepts of Yahweh and Elohim until these collections of ideas about God would be as intimate to him as recollections of his own father; to analyze and understand the oracles about the messiah until they were second nature to him; and then, at the proper time, to announce his mission to his people with the authority of the prophets of old. John went to the wilderness, to the dry and barren desert country of Judea; for a time he went to the regimen of the Essene community at Qumran, then to the lonely places of the Sinai where Moses himself encountered God long ago as the present participle of the verb "to be," and to the denial of the self which John believed would produce spiritual power. When they were ready, the young men had said, they would meet again and renew the covenant between them. It was a grand scheme, of the kind young men dream, and forget. But Jesus and John did not forget, and they proved to be tough-minded in the pursuit of their dream in a way their enemies would underestimate until the very end.

Some years later the people flocked to John's preaching, rough and eccentric as he had become. Jesus knew the time had come for him too. He went to John, heard him with approval, and was baptized by him. Both men knew their enterprise was blessed by God. The people responded gladly to their preaching. A popular religious movement began.

There was a difference between the cousins now, however, even more than before. John the Baptist recognized and submitted to the authority of Jesus' person. They both had paid the price of the knowledge of God, but Jesus had been given some special power.

Then an event happened which profoundly affected their covenant and their lives. John the Baptist was arrested and imprisoned for criticizing the tetrarch Herod's relations with his brother's wife Herodias. A few months later John was beheaded. Jesus had hoped to avoid this kind of political intrigue. The formal religious leaders of the nation lived by clandestine stratagems. It was the reason they were out of favor with the people. Jesus would have been more circumspect than John. Such quarreling as he had to do was with the Sadducees and Pharisees, not the politicians. It was obvious now, however, that he had to take the political structure into account. He would soon learn that his religious opponents had political alliances he could not ignore either.

He would have to rethink his career. Perhaps he would have to resort to his knowledge of David to accomplish his mission. At any rate he had a briefer time than he had hoped.

Jesus worked out his contingency plan in the time called the Temptation. He would not engage evil at the political level for the time being. He would eventually share John's fate, that much was clear. But he would pick the time, place and circumstances of his own arrest and death. He could not repeat John's mistake and be summarily put away before the planting of the Lord had been completed. His whole life, what was left of it, had to become a carefully orchestrated event. He had to teach in such a way that the common people would remember his words. He had to leave mighty deeds behind. He had to fend off the authorities until the people knew who he was. He had to stay away from Jerusalem until he was ready to confront the whole power structure of the society, and then he would be ready to die.

Jesus would make of those last days in Jerusalem a celebration of the scripture and all he had learned about the suffering servant. He would enter Jerusalem as a king, but on a donkey, not a steed. Let them figure that one out. He would cleanse the temple. He would use powerful symbols and a liturgy to call a remembering community into being. He would himself become a guilt offering and a pascal lamb. All of this would take place at the Passover three years from now, the ancient

Feast of Liberation, when another believing community had been called into being long ago. Jesus would not die in ignominy as John had. He would die in triumph as he fulfilled the oracles. He would become the true Son of David.

To do all of this and to improvise along the way, Jesus had to live out the truth of Kierkegaard's dictum that purity of heart is to will one thing. He had to give up responsibility for his younger brothers and sisters, left in his keeping when his father died years ago. He had to bear the pain of his mother's grief for him. He had to abandon the other Mary, whom he loved so much. He had to move to Capernaum, where he would be safe, and gather a few trusted friends. Later he would have to manipulate events in Jerusalem. He would find a way.

Jesus assumed John's mantle and preach-
ed repentance. He went back to Galilee
to do it, however, staying out of reach
of the authorities. In his home synagogue in Nazareth, Jesus announced
his mission by reading these words
from the prophet Isaiah:
    "The Spirit of the Lord is upon me,
    because he has anointed me to
        preach good news to the poor.
    He has sent me to proclaim
        release to the captives.
    and recovering of sight to the blind,
    to set at liberty those who
        are oppressed,
    to proclaim the acceptable year
        of the Lord."
Jesus then said to his fellow worship-
pers:"Today this scripture has been

fulfilled in your hearing." It was an audacious thing to do, but the people of Nazareth accepted him in his role as prophet, at least until he started meddling.

Jesus went around the countryside proclaiming the coming of the Kingdom of God. He raised from the death of parental suffocation the son of the widow of Nain and the daughter of Jairus. He healed those who had decided they could not walk or see. He forgave those who believed themselves to be unforgivable. He said the possession of money, power, and preferment had nothing to do with happiness. He celebrated friendship, peace, birds, and flowers, and he said that a little was enough. He freed people from the tyranny of the law, teaching that the only law which mattered is the love of

God and the love of one's neighbor.

Such apostasy of course brought inquiries and visitors from Jerusalem. Jesus watched the circle of his freedom tighten as agents from the Sanhedrin arrived. He knew his popular following was buying him time. He also became aware that he had friends in the Sanhedrin, a few men of learning who recognized in Jesus an authentic voice from Israel's past. They admired him for being a brilliant raconteur. But their messages counseled discretion. They advised the consideration of incremental change. They suggested taking the longer look. "Do not be a meteor across the night sky," they said. "You have more class than the Baptist; use your intelligence and wit to become part of us, the cognoscenti. In the

end we are the preservers."

Jesus never wavered. Instead he knew now how to accomplish his purposes in Jerusalem. Potentially he had the allies, the inside men, he needed. He would use them: John the Priest, Nicodemus, and Joseph of Arimathea, all members of the Council itself. That is how David would have done it. And he could count on Judas Iscariot to do anything he asked. Judas had long believed the movement needed a martyr to succeed.

The drama intensified. Jesus was increasingly enraged by the hard-heartedness and hypocrisy of most of the religious leaders of his day. His language was more and more scornful as he described them. His humanity was strained by the knowledge that he could not compromise with them,

that his earlier desire merely to purify Judaism must now have some other end, and that the success of the end game of this chess match hung only by the thread of his own will. He was alone, and he was afraid.

Jesus traveled secretly to Jerusalem in October under cover of the activity of the Feast of Tabernacles to make preparations for next spring's Passover, when he would force a confrontation with the chief priests. He asked John the Priest to call a meeting in John's house near the temple itself. Jesus outlined his strategy, as David the general would have done. He would make his headquarters at the home of Lazarus and Lazarus' sisters Mary and Martha in Bethany, barely three miles across the Kidron valley from the temple, but too far away for a surprise arrest. Jesus would have to make several trips into the city, the first as the triumphal Son of David to bring taut his challenge to the hierarchy, then daily to cleanse and teach in the temple itself, all in the open and all in the light of day, protected by his popular following. On Thursday evening Jesus would use this same upper room in John's house to eat the Passover meal with his disciples. Thursday night Judas would lead the authorities to a private place in the Garden of Gethsemane where Jesus would be arrested without resistance. John the Priest, Nicodemus, and Joseph would have to keep Jesus informed of the ebb and flow of debate in the Council. There could be no surprises.

The men nodded their understanding and their agreement. Here was a brave Galilean who knew his days were numbered. Rather than die in a prison or by an assassin's hand, he was choosing to die as part of a memorable drama, as a King, but also as a sacrifice, as the lamb of God. He believed his death would be redemptive. It was a bold and noble plan. "He deserves our pity and our help," they thought. The men agreed on a communication system and Jesus returned to Galilee.

During the winter that followed the agreement, the Jerusalem connection was more and more impressed with the truth of Jesus' teaching as it was reported by agents of the Council. They discussed among themselves the psychoanalytic power of his personality, his command of the scripture, the way he appeared to be living out the prophesies about the messiah, but how much of a heretic he was, especially in his treatment of the unclean. Those pithy sayings of his were hard to forget: "You shall know the truth and the truth shall make you free." Joseph of Arimathea became a secret disciple. Nicodemus argued Jesus' case in the Council. John the Priest conceived a variation on Jesus' plan which at first boggled the minds of the other players in the end game drama.

John got the idea on a visit to Qumran, where he had gone to see his old friend, Eleazar. He always visited Eleazar when he was deeply troubled. He also knew that

John the Baptist had spent his adolescent years at Qumran before he became an independent prophet. Given the strange bond between Jesus and the Baptist, perhaps Eleazar could help him understand what was going on here.

Eleazar saw that his young and well-born friend was reflective enough that he might hear something about the wellsprings of the thought of Jesus and John. "It has to do with oneness and the life to come," Eleazar said. "The life to come is simply a life of quality that some people begin while they yet live, but it is difficult for others to understand the concept. Past, present, and future are all one. The sacred and the profane are one. God is the God of evil as well as the good. In fact he encompasses evil and allows it to be. Work and play are experienced as the same thing. The spoken and the unspoken prayer are both heard. Success and failure are both imposters, because life is justified outside the self. The one who justifies life does make occasional and unexpected incursions on present selves, however, and what we do here at Qumran is stay ready to recognize the visitations of God when they come. Jesus is quite possibly a visitation from God, at least his cousin John thought so."

John the Priest sat there slowly comprehending. Then passionately he asked why Jesus should be allowed to die before others knew the truth he carried. Eleazar replied that they could not prevent it, that any power structure, political or religious, could not long suffer the embarrassment of the exposure of its institutional norms. John the Priest did not accept the rationale. "Can we not this once prolong the life of the good? Must we always grovel in this martyr complex which even Jesus seems to share? Can we not just one time outdo the enemies of righteousness and thus honor God? Jesus needs more time."

John the Priest found his mark in the old man, something cavalier and proud from long ago. His reply was a curious one. "Have you heard of the sons of Baruch? They were resuscitated after crucifixion two years ago. The Romans broke their legs on the cross, the way they always do, so the victims will never walk again, but their friends got them down before they died. They are alive today. There are other cases, too, but no one likes to advertise them."

The facile mind of John the Priest flew like a computer across the possibilities. The timing was right. Jesus would be arrested Thursday night. With some engineering by John in the Council, the trial could be summarily held, and Jesus could be on the cross by mid-morning Friday. The Romans always allowed the Jews to take victims down by the start of the Sabbath at sundown Friday, especially if Jewish leaders insisted on it. Joseph of Arimathea could ask for Jesus' body and put it in a tomb near the crucifixion site at Golgotha. Normally it took a victim longer than a few hours to die from the asphyxiation of his body hanging from its wrists, but if Jesus appeared to be dead, the centurion in charge would probably be cooperative. If he appeared to be dead before the breaking of the legs, which came toward the end of the crucifixion process and hastened death by making the body sag more on the cross, Jesus could even walk again. A group of women sobbing at the scene would be a good diversion, and their milling around when the body was placed in a burial shroud would make it easier to dress Jesus' wounds. As soon as it was safe Friday night, Jesus' body could be retrieved from the tomb and brought to Qumran for resuscitation. They could bribe anyone they had to.

There was a medical problem, of course, said the teamed computer in John's brain. How could Jesus appear to be dead? Could he withstand the agony of writhing on a cross for nine hours? He would be scourged before the spikes were nailed into his wrists and feet. How much would they beat him? Could Jesus' friends get to him in the tomb before the appearance of death became a reality? The real problem, however, would probably be Jesus himself. He would not agree to this variation on his plan. He wanted the grandstand play, the purity of the liturgical act. But maybe they could convince him. The advantages were obvious: he could take the worst punishment the religious and political authorities could impose on him, and come back from it. They would leave him alone after that for sure. Perhaps he would accept a compromise: he could beat the crucifixion all right, but not go public again. He could stay in Qumran and teach a generation of eager young people the ways of right-eousness.

Eleazar heard the plan and nodded his admiration of it, although John the Priest sensed that Eleazar knew something about it he did not know. John's doubt was dispelled as Eleazar took him to see the two medical experts of the Essene community. They assured John there was indeed a mixture, a narcotic, which could be administered orally to bring a patient quickly into deep unconciousness, with barely a discernible heartbeat. And, yes, they would attend Jesus. John returned to Jerusalem to convince the others of the justice of his cause.

The principal action of this drama took place in a single two-week period in the early spring of the year 30 A.D. Significantly, the Passover that year also fell on the Sabbath, April 8. In addition to meeting the requirements of his public ministry, Jesus had spent the previous winter reviewing his knowledge of ancient Jewish ritual and the Biblical affirmations of God's perpetual covenant with David. In his mind Jesus would become the burnt offering, the cereal offering, the peace offering, the sin offering, the guilt offering, and the scapegoat, all focused into one human being. In his sacrificial death he would bring atonement, at-one-ment, to his fragmented people.

They had so many laws to worry about that spontaneity had been sapped from their lives. He would make it possible for them once again to have the direct experience of the mercies of God. He would bear their sins on the cross.

In his childhood Jesus had sung many of the songs attributed to David. Some of them were about God's coming salvation. In fact one of the Hebrew prayers of Jesus' time, which he recited regularly at worship, was the entreaty to God to "Speedily cause the branch of David, thy servant, to sprout, and let his horn be exalted by thy salvation; because daily do we wait for thy salvation." Jesus now saw himself as the sprouting branch. He was the instrument of salvation. He was the Son of David.

The knowledge almost paralyzed him. It used to be just a fantasy, but there is nothing in the young man's messiah about the suffering servant. The messiah for the young of whatever chronological age is "a leader and commander of the people." It is true that David suffered. His early life had been endangered by the reigning monarch, Saul, so that he was forced to lead the precarious existence of a hunted outlaw. There had been many other trials and tribulations. But God did save David from death at the hands of his enemies. The promise was fulfilled that David would reign over all Israel, and he was assured that his line would endure forever. God even promised to be a father to him.

In his own coming of age, Jesus

knew beyond any doubt that the messiah
of the prophets would be called upon to
give up his life. Now he would have to
face the awful technical reality of his
adult fantasy's accomplishment in
Jerusalem. Having no weapons but his
sense of history and drama, he would
play the royal and sacral king. It gave
him some grim and amused satisfac-
tion that he would go to his death
in a memorable style and for a purpose worthy of him. He reviewed the
plan once more: he would be anointed in Bethany; he would enter Jerusalem in triumph; he would make
the temple precincts his own; he
would confront the power structure
in uncompromising dignity; he would
shock the people and those who remembered the event into committing their
cause to God and turning back to him

in faith and repentance.

It would have been easier if anyone among his family and friends understood. After the death of his father when Jesus was fourteen, there had been no one in the world in whom he could confide. Even the other Mary, who laughingly used to refer to herself as "your Bathsheba" still demanded that he be normal. She would be among the group of women following him to Jerusalem for the showdown. The tradeoffs had been his choice however. The intelligentsia were not in the backwaters of Galilee, but neither were the cynics. The innocence of the uncalculating personalities around him had given him the time he needed to develop his message, and the fishermen would have the capacity someday to believe. He had had to be

watchful from the day he returned to Galilee from the Jordon valley, saying and doing nothing the spies and informers could seize upon as seditious. He had to pray and meditate and chart his course. Loneliness was part of the bargain.

It was time. Before Jesus began his trek south, to arrive in Jerusalem six days before the Passover, as he had agreed with the Jerusalem connection, he left the safety of Capernaum to walk thirty miles north to Caesarea Philippi. Jesus sought the perspective of nearby Mount Hermon, 8,500 feet high. There he received the confirmation he needed. Almost three years earlier, on another journey of faith, he had felt his baptism by John blessed by the spirit of God. The authenticating words were: "Thou art my beloved son; with thee I am well pleased." Now on Mount Hermon three of the disciples thought they saw Jesus transfigured and in con-

versation with Moses and Elijah, Moses representing the ancient law, and Elijah the tradition of the prophets. The words the disciples thought they heard were similar to those of the baptism: "This is my beloved son; listen to him." Jesus had chosen the right course. Peter recognized that, too, inarticulate as he was, and proclaimed Jesus to be the messiah. Perhaps fishermen were not as ignorant as some thought.

The company stopped by its base at Capernaum as Jesus set his face steadfastly toward Jerusalem. He warned his followers of what lay ahead: "Think not that I am come to send peace on earth. I come not to send peace, but a sword." He hurled difficult sayings at his friends making ready for the pilgrimage. He de-

manded an emotional commitment to an unnatural and irrational standard of conduct: the rupture of family ties, the abnegation of personal freedom, and the surrender of one's will. Jesus brooked neither discussion nor doubt on these subjects. It was his fanatical side, which people would remember alongside his kindness and the compassion he showed for children, the sick and elderly, and the poor and needy.

The band made its way south to Judea. Large crowds followed. Jesus continued to heal and to draw object lessons with his parables. Pharisees continued to test him for orthodoxy. Progress was slow. They entered Jericho on Thursday, March 30. The town was barely fifteen miles from Jerusalem, and it was a fair day.

Jericho was a place of orchards and gardens. It bore crops year after year: bananas, pomegranates, almonds, oranges, and dates with the savor of honey. Jesus and his disciples walked through this paradise and breathed the aroma of balsam. In the orchards peasants gashed the balsam with sharp stones and collected the sap in bowls, where it quickly thickened into the gum of golden red myrrh.

A blind man shouted, "Son of David, have pity on me!" Jesus stopped. "Call him here," he said. Bartimaeus the Beggar threw off his cloak, jumped up, and ran toward the voice. "What do you want me to do for you?" Jesus asked. "Master, let me see again." Jesus said, "Go. Your faith has saved you." Bartimaeus' sight returned. Thus it was, over and over

again. People came to Jesus and became what they believed they could become. Salvation also came to Zacchaeus that day in Jericho. He was a tax collector and a wealthy and hated man with whom Jesus chose to spend the night. Zacchaeus responded to Jesus' recognition of his humanity by giving half his property to the poor. It was such an unusual act for a man of wealth the disciples wondered if the inauguration of the Kingdom of God was at hand.

The disciples had been extraordinarily patient. They had lived with Jesus day after day, observing him in exultation and despair. They knew his mother and brothers and sisters. They rejoiced in the sublime manifestations of his greatness of soul, and they endured his violent

outbursts of anger. They were not always respectful and not always persuaded. But now, just maybe, their hopes would be realized and the people of Israel would be awakened from their sloth. Yes, these were fair days.

The group moved on to Bethany the next day before the Sabbath began at sundown. Jesus was to stay the final week of his life here at the home of Lazarus and Lazarus' sisters, Mary and Martha. Jesus would be anointed here, not by a prophet or a high priest, or the commander of his army, but by the girl, Mary. She would shock the pragmatists by the extravagance of her love as she poured pure nard on Jesus' feet and dried them with her hair. It was a coronation.

Tonight Jesus would have his conversation with Judas. Judas was a complex man, but Jesus understood him. He was essentially a man of detail, believing God was in the details. He was treasurer of the disciples' group. He was also fiercely loyal to Jesus and to the messianic ideal which he knew Jesus represented. He was the only non-Galilean among the disciples, and he was coming home now to Judea. This was his territory. He knew every passageway of the Holy City. The qualities about Judas which Jesus counted on were his intensity, his sense of discipline and duty, his willingness to sacrifice, and a love for Jesus comparable to that of the champions of David the king. Judas did not count the cost, though frequently he paid it when due.

Jesus began the conversation with an explanation of Mary's anointing which would take place in a few hours. It would be an anointing for burial as well as for kingship. Judas nodded his understanding with tears in his eyes, but they were not allowed to run down his cheeks. The two men had talked before about how death can further certain causes of life. For the first time outside the Jerusalem circle Jesus spoke of the ritualistic aspect of every significant event in the week about to begin. He told Judas about the arrangements for the donkey, the entry into Jerusalem, the temple appearance to force the Council's hand, his friends in the Council itself, the timing associated with the preparation of the sacrifice, the celebration of the Passover meal in the home of John the Priest, the arrest, the trial, and his death, probably on a Roman cross if the Council was successful in charging him with treason. He entrusted Judas with the whole plan.

Someone had to go to the chief priests and tell them Jesus was ready to surrender. After the triumphal entry tomorrow, that would be welcome news. Someone had to lead them to Jesus in Gethsemane in the darkness of Thursday night. Someone from Jesus' company had to see to it that the schedule was kept, not their schedule, but Jesus' schedule. "I need a liaison, Judas, and a listening post. Will you do it?"

It was a dagger thrust into Judas' heart. "I, Jesus? I love you best of all. You have always known that!"

"Yes, Judas, I know. That is why I ask you to help me fulfill my purpose."

"I will be misunderstood by our friends."

"Yes. Each of us has a role to play in this drama, and neither of us chose the genetics of his casting. Suppose we give it up Judas, this good thing we do, and go home to live....how many more years? Ten? Twenty? Will the quality of those years outweigh the greater opportunity we have now to make our lives count? I think not. Let us seize the opportunity we have to liberate our people. Our mutual sacrifice will do that."

Judas hesitated. He considered Jesus' words and then embraced him as he would again in the Garden. He asked for further details of Jesus' plan. He would play his part, because he loved Jesus best of all.

The next morning, April 2, Jesus set out with his entourage toward Bethphage, a suburb of Jerusalem. Soon he sent two disciples to get his charger, the king's stallion, and to make contact with John the Priest. Other than Judas, the disciples did not know the identity of Jesus' collaborator. Security was important. The donkey was where Jesus said it would be, and the owner said what Jesus said he would say: "Why are you untying it?" The disciples' reply said all was well. "The master has need of it."

The rest of the day was like that fair day in Jericho, only more exhilarating. Jesus and the disciples

joined with the other pilgrims going along the road to the Passover festival. Jesus' reputation preceded him. The crowd ran into the fields and cut foliage to lay in the roadway before him. They spread their garments on the road as the people had done before King Jehu centuries ago shouting: "Jehu is King." Now the people shouted: "Hosanna to the Son of David! Blessed is he who comes in the name of the Lord! Hosanna in the highest!" The pilgrims danced and sang for two miles.

Thus Jesus entered Jerusalem as a conqueror on a donkey. It was high comedy and could only have happened in that strange Godplace, Israel, with its longstanding love affair with the improbable. The city was genuinely stirred. Even the

inattentive asked who caused this tumult. The crowd answered, "This is the prophet Jesus from Nazareth of Galilee." The urbanites sniffed that he probably spoke with that horrible northern accent. It was the reaction of the Council that counted, however. The Council knew what Jesus had done. He had challenged them in their fortress, and he would have to be dealt with. That would not be easy with this popular following of his. He was a worthy adversary.

Jesus came back from Bethany each day for the next three days, overturning the tables of the money-changers in the temple, attacking the Pharisees unmercifully, teaching on many subjects before great crowds, and daring the authorities to inter-cept him. Judas' offer to the chief

priests was a curious but welcome one, curious because a player as circumspect as Judas would not betray his principal at the height of his game, and welcome because it solved the problem of how to lay hold of Jesus without a riot. Jesus' popular appeal in the meantime convinced John the Priest, Nicodemus, and Joseph of Arimathea, if they needed any more convincing, that they could not allow him to throw his life away.

It was John who pulled Jesus aside on Tuesday evening near Solomon's porch and asked to walk back toward Bethany with him, to stop on the Mount of Olives opposite the temple. "You should not be seen with me," said Jesus. John answered, "You have enough informers around you trying to get evidence. I might as well try too.

Besides, I might be able to straighten you out." Jesus smiled and said, "Let's go."

They talked long after the temple was a silhouette against the evening sky. Jesus was fascinated by the resuscitation plan. He loved John for the genius and motives of it. His humanity strained in him as it would several times that week, as when he prayed in Gethsemane: "Father, if it be possible let this cup pass from me." Jesus did not want to die. He wanted to allow himself to love Mary as she still loved him. He wanted to enjoy his friends and use his power to heal. He yearned to consider the lilies of the field and the birds of the air, but he was trapped by obedience. Of all people, John, as a priest, should have understood

the learnings to come from the role-play of the ritual of the suffering servant: the saving power of the symbols and their lasting effect.

John was not surprised that Jesus rejected the Passover plot. Jesus had his own Passover plot. John would execute his anyway. He would save Jesus from himself. When Jesus was brought back to health at Qumran he would thank him. Who did Jesus think he was, anyway, God? Only God saves and has lasting effect.

It was only chance, well, not entirely by chance, that Judas overheard the last part of John's report to Nicodemus and Joseph the next day. As Jesus' communication link, he had gone to the triumvirate Wednesday afternoon to get a report of the Sanhedrin's morning meeting.

Did the Council believe Judas? Had consensus been reached? Was the arrest and trial agreed to? Was the triumvirate able to finesse an early Friday morning appearance before the Council and pave the way for the other judgments which had to be made in rapid succession? The answer was in the affirmative to these questions and others, but as Judas was out of sight he also heard John's anguished outburst, "He won't do it." The rest of what Judas heard gnawed at his soul even as his heart leaped at John's alternative. He wanted to join forces with these good men and save Jesus. But he could not. He had to help Jesus fulfill his purpose.

Judas went straight to Caiaphas, the High Priest. This time he did betray. He betrayed three men who had

befriended Jesus, but who now stood in the way of Jesus' triumph. Caiaphas weighed Judas' information. The silencing of Jesus was too important for him to abort the arrangements already made in the Council for Jesus' removal. A way had to be found to assure Jesus' death on the cross despite the drug which would make him appear to be dead. Jesus would still have to come down from the cross by sunset. Caiaphas pondered the matter and assured Judas he would handle it. It would be best for all parties in the accommodation, and for the purposes of each set of actors, including Jesus, that this matter be kept between Caiaphas and Judas. Judas agreed.

One did not bribe centurions of a Roman legion, not this centurion anyway. Marcellus did respond to a discreet inquiry about who would be in the execution detail on Friday, however. Caiaphas found his man. Late in the crucifixion process, just before sundown, the soldier would put a spear in Jesus' side and end the plot. The conspirators had not counted on that. The soldier would also see to it that Jesus had a more savage scourging than was usually the case, to weaken him more. The traitors would be deprived of their resurrection, the Council would be relieved of its annoyance, and Jesus would serve whatever purpose he thought his death would accomplish.

Thursday, April 6, was the last full day of Jesus' life. He prayed for the power of will to make the day count. It was the first day of Unleavened Bread in the ancient Jewish religion, when the Passover lamb was sacrificed. The rules governing the celebration were explicit. During the day a male animal without blemish was to be taken from the flock and ritualistically slaughtered, with some of the animal's blood put on the two doorposts and the lintel of the house of the believer. That night the flesh of the sacrifice would be "roasted over the fire, eaten with unleavened bread and bitter herbs." It was called the Passover in honor of Yahweh, the Lord God, because later that night

long ago Yahweh had gone through the land of Egypt and struck down all the first-born, passing over the houses marked with the blood of the lamb. It was proclaimed a day of remembrance for Israel. "For all generations you are to declare it a day of festival forever." The Passover symbolized Israel's readiness to depart, to go into any wilderness.

Despite Jesus' quarrel with ultra-orthodox Jews over their legalistic attitude toward the Mosaic Code, he scrupulously followed the normal Jewish observances. It was natural that his disciples should ask him on this day how they would observe the Passover meal. Again the previous arrangements with John the Priest came into play. Jesus told Peter and

John the son of Zebedee to go into the city where, by the gate near the pool, they would be met by a man carrying a water-pot. Normally women went to draw water, so they could easily pick the man out. They were to follow him to the house he would enter, go in themselves, and say to the owner, "The master says, which guest room am I to have to eat the Passover with my disciples?" They would then be shown a large upstairs room already laid out, where they were to prepare the Passover meal. Jesus' carefully arranged plans were followed to the letter. He came to John's house himself later that evening with the other disciples for the pascal meal.

The age-old service, the seder, began. Jesus recited the blessing over the first of the four obligatory cups

of wine of the evening, and handed it on for the disciples to share. He told them he was inaugurating the Kingdom of God. Such a saying seemed less strange now than similar ones had before. As the meal progressed, Jesus signaled Judas to go for the Civil Guard.

Eventually Jesus broke the last bread of the evening and distributed pieces to the disciples, telling them it signified his body. After grace he took the third cup of wine, known as "the cup of blessing," recited the benediction, and passed it around saying, "This signifies the new covenant in my blood, which is poured out for many." The service concluded with the drinking of the fourth cup of wine and the chanting of several psalms. In that moment the Passover became the Eucharist.

This simple supper provided the early Church with its basic act of worship, already practiced in the time of the Apostle Paul, barely twenty years after the event. The essential theme was a man offering his physical existence, his flesh and blood, in order that other men and women might experience a spiritual existence which would unite them with the ground of their being.

Jesus was ready to submit himself to the cross. He embraced John the Priest, his host, and led the remaining eleven disciples out into the street, out of the city across the Kidron valley to the Garden of Gethsemane on the lower slopes of the Mount of Olives. As they proceeded Jesus warned the disciples they would waver in their loyalty, quoting the prophet Zechariah: "I will strike at the shepherd, and the sheep will be scattered." Peter responded stoutly that even if everyone else ran, he would not. Jesus stopped abruptly at that point and looked at Peter forever: "Simon, Simon," he said, "Satan has begged to have you that he may pry you loose like husks from the grain. But I have prayed that your loyalty will not fail. On your restoration you must confirm your brothers." Peter would remember that.

Now, however, Peter remonstrated, "In your cause, Master, I am ready to go to prison and to death too."

Jesus shook his head. "I tell you for a fact, Peter, the cock will not crow today before you have denied three times that you even know me."

When they got to Gethsemane Jesus confessed to them all that he was in very low spirits. Until tonight he had regarded the physical suffering in store for him almost impersonally. There had been a certain grandeur about it, a kind of glorious calculation, which excused him from the details of what he must experience. Now it was different. The hour had come. Did he have the strength and fortitude to die well under torture? Could he stand up to his inquisitors with dignity and some measure of grace?

While Jesus was praying for strength, his friends fell asleep. The meal they had eaten and the wine they had drunk proved too much for them. Jesus was completely alone. There was no human prop on which to lean, no friend on earth to whom he could turn as he faced his ordeal.

Judas arrived with the force dispatched by the Council. With the Civil Guard were several servants of the chief priests. Judas had given instructions to secure the man he would embrace. Jesus said something to Judas while Judas held him, but no one was sure what. The disciples scattered, unpursued by the Guard. It was Jesus they wanted.

The prisoner was taken first before Annas, former high priest and head of the most powerful sacerdotal family of the time. He was also the father-in-law of the reigning high priest, Caiaphas. Annas questioned Jesus closely about his teaching and following. Annas wanted to know primarily if there was a popular uprising afoot. Jesus flatly denied that he was engaged in any subversive activity. What he taught had been spoken openly and publicly. "Why do you ask me?" Jesus replied to a question. "Ask those who listened to what I said to them. They know what I said."

Jesus was cuffed by a guard for his insolence, but the shrewd Annas judged he was sincere. This would be easier than it might have been. Annas

sent Jesus on to the Council, manacled and closely escorted. It was only necessary to have Jesus executed and whatever was brewing would be stopped. The man was clearly a deluded fanatic.

The Sanhedrin met in special session in the small hours of that Friday morning not so much to try Jesus as to find grounds on which to formulate an indictment that would procure from the Roman governor the condemnation of Jesus to summary execution. The Council could not have succeeded in that objective if Jesus had not wanted it to. His theology could not be at issue. The penalty for theological wrongdoing, blasphemy, was stoning, and even then the offender could not be stoned to death. The Romans had denied the Council permission to impose the death penalty. The issue had to be Jesus'

political pretensions. It was hard to make a political charge stick, though, because Jesus had been so circumspect in his public utterances. To make matters worse, as the debate went on, Jesus remained silent. Once again he was determined to fulfill prophecy: "As a sheep before her shearers is dumb, so he opened not his mouth." John, Nicodemus, and Joseph watched Jesus with unbridled admiration. If there was ever an opportunity to rage against the darkness, and make fools of these jackals, this was it.

The high priest challenged Jesus directly. "Have you no answer to make to these charges?" Jesus said nothing. The only hope for Caiaphas was to force Jesus to incriminate himself. Caiaphas bluntly put the question to him on oath: "Are you the messiah?"

This time Jesus answered. "Yes, I am." He waited for the smiles of relief and victory to go around the room, and then reiterated that dimension of his messiahship they did not understand: "Hereafter you will see the Son of Man sitting on the right hand of power, and coming with the clouds of heaven." To the Council, Jesus' impudence was not unlike Patrick Henry saying to the King of England, "If this be treason, make the most of it."

The high priest rent his tunic, a formal sign of sorrow. "What further evidence do we need?" he cried. "You have heard his traitorous confession. What is your decision?" The Council judged Jesus to be deserving of the death penalty. By claiming he was the messiah, the Son of David, the rightful and foreordained king of Israel, Jesus had committed a blasphemy all right,

not of God in Jewish law, but of Tiberius Caesar in Roman law. He was guilty, they held, of _laesa maiestas_, violation of the emperor's sovereignty. It was therefore proper for the scandalized authorities, not as Jews but as Roman subjects, to act as _delatores_ and inform against Jesus to Caesar's representative.

Jesus had not declared himself to be divine. Once again, as he had throughout his public career, Jesus declared himself to be the Son of Man: representative man, a man seeking God's heart as David had done. The Council knew it did not have cause to condemn Jesus on religious grounds. On religious grounds the Jewish people approved of Jesus heartily. He was another prophet, which was precisely the problem. The Sadducees, who made up a majority of the Council, had long since subordinated their re-

ligious sensibilities to the requirements of position. They clung to inherited prestige and habits of luxurious living by intrigue and cooperation with the Roman occupation forces to keep the people subdued. The Pharisees had taken another route equally irresponsible in the mind of Jesus. They were preoccupied with the details of the Mosaic Law. They insisted that every jot and tittle of the law be obeyed. Monitoring the legal process took so much of their energy that little was left for spontaneity and the direct experience of God. The Pharisees felt that every important issue could be reduced to a legal determination. The Romans approved of this philosophy of life, of course, because as long as the Pharisaic party was preoccupied with religious observances, it would not be fomenting revolution.

The Council's greatest fear from the beginning was a popular demonstration in Jesus' favor. Its motives were those of self-preservation and self interest. What else would explain this extraordinary meeting before dawn? The Sadducees knew they walked a tightrope. They were out of favor with the Jewish masses and were able to offer their Roman masters only a debased coin of temporary stability. Not long after Jesus' appearance before the Council, Caiaphas was deposed from office by Vitellius, the legate of Syria. Within forty years of this scene the palaces of the Sadducaic nobility would be sacked by mobs, and the chief priests would be hunted down and killed. The popular revolt the Council had feared so much would begin in 66 A.D. and continue for seven bloody years. Jerusalem and the tem-

ple would be destroyed in 70 A.D., and the Jewish state would cease to exist shortly after that, not to be restored until 1948 A.D. The eschatological vision of Jesus had been an accurate reading of the seeds of destruction being sown by the Sanhedrin's abdication of the responsibility to govern during the first half of the first century.

Now the Council acted to rid itself of its annoyance, and it did so before the city awakened to what was going on. As early as possible after sunrise on Friday, Jesus was brought before the Roman governor, Pontius Pilate. The indictment formulated by the Council was in purely political terms. "We have found this man subverting our nation, forbidding the

payment of tribute to Caesar, and claiming to be the messiah, a king." It was a capital crime.

Pilate was suspicious. He did not trust these people, and it was unnatural that the chief priests should be accusing a fellow Jew of conspiracy against Rome. The man standing before him did not look like a revolutionary.

Pilate asked Jesus, "Are you the king of the Jews?" He expected a denial or an indication that the prisoner was a harmless lunatic. Instead he got a calm, conversational inquiry, equal speaking to equal: "Are you asking this of your own accord, or did others suggest it to you about me?"

"Am I a Jew?" roared Pilate. "Your own people, the chief priests, have handed you over to me. What have you done?"

Jesus had been up all night and under great strain, but he was remarkably clear-headed and articulate. He explained that his kingdom did not belong to the existing world order. Had it been otherwise his followers would have fought to save him from arrest. Then the old insolence crept in. How could the messianic kingdom be made intelligible to a heathen Roman official? It was quite beyond Pilate's comprehension.

Pilate did not overreact. He admired Jesus' courage. He knew he was talking to a man of parts, and he was less angry than amused. "You are a king, then?"

"I am a king, as you say." Jesus answered, not amused at all. He might have added, "And you must help me come into my kingdom." Instead Jesus was enigmatic again: "I was born and

came into the world to witness to the truth. All who heed the truth listen to me."

"What does truth mean?" Pilate asked thoughtfully, and then went out to the waiting accusers. "I find nothing against him," he told them shortly.

The whole enterprise hung in the balance. The chief priests pressed their charges: "He rouses the people, teaching all over Judea, beginning with Galilee and ending up here."

Galilee? "Ah," thought Pilate, "Here is a way to get rid of this ghastly business. Jesus is a Galilean. The tetrarch of Galilee is in Jerusalem for the Passover and is staying at the Hasmonean Palace along the hill." Pilate told the chief priests to take Jesus to Herod Antipas for judgment.

It did not work. Herod ques-

INRI

INRI

tioned Jesus at length and returned him to Pilate with a message that he was harmless.

The chief priests realized they would have to bring heavy pressure on Pilate, so they packed the courtyard of the praetorium with their agents and slaves. The crowd shouted and milled around. Someone made the sinister accusation: "If you free this man you are no friend of Caesar's. Whoever claims to be a king is in opposition to Caesar."

That did it. Pilate could not have that kind of gossip getting back to Rome. He had enough trouble with the gossip that was true. So Pilate condemned Jesus to be crucified, although he symbolically washed his hands of personal responsibility for the death of a man innocent of the charges against him. "We are all guilty of something," thought Pilate. The chief priests had their way. They had browbeaten the governor into compliance.

Jesus was flogged. He was thrashed an excessive number of times with metal-tipped whips which tore out pieces of his flesh. The execution detail decked the prisoner out as a mock king with a crimson cloak around his shoulders and a wreath on his head that was a clump of thorns digging into his scalp. He had to carry his own cross to the place of execution, bending under the weight of it and suffering deep abrasions on his shoulders. Then three spikes were nailed into his body, one through each wrist, and one through his over-

lapped feet. Crucifixion required the victim to writhe on the cross in torment until gradually his body was asphyxiated.

The crosses of Jesus and two others were hoisted up on Golgotha and the victims suspended on them before Jerusalem had awakened to the business at hand. Pilate had some revenge though, for himself and for Jesus. He had the Council's charge posted above Jesus' cross: "King of the Jews." He refused to change the wording to "He said, I am King of the Jews."

Jesus clung grimly to his role-play as messiah. On the cross he began the recitation of the 22nd Psalm, one of David's cries of anguish: "My God, my God, why hast thou forsaken me?" He continued the psalm silently until the end: "All this he has done," which

**INRI**

would be translated in John's Gospel:
"It is finished."

Jesus passed the messianic tests.
He carried out the exacting stipulations
of the oracles. The task to which he had
applied his mind and heart was concluded. Lifted up as an ensign
to the nations, he reigned on
the cross as the Son of David.

Not all of Jerusalem had been asleep that previous night. John the Priest had been one of the chief priests in attendance at all the goings-on, more determined than ever to defeat Jesus' enemies. When someone had raised to Jesus' lips a sponge saturated with wine vinegar late in the afternoon of the crucifixion, the sponge had also contained the narcotic the Essenes had brought from Egypt. Soon after tasting it Jesus slipped into oblivion.

Marcellus had seen many men die, though none with quite the spirit of this one. As evening came and the time neared to remove the body from the cross, the centurion declined to have the victim's legs broken, since Jesus was apparently already dead.

He was enraged when Felix reached up with his lance and unnecessarily thrust it into Jesus' side, so that blood and water streamed out. Marcellus reprimanded the soldier, demanding to know why he must further defile this admirable man. Felix was rather stupid, though, a good soldier whose life had been brutalized long ago.

From the distance Caiaphas sighed relief. Judas remembered that God was in the details. John the Priest, Nicodemus, and Joseph of Arimathea recoiled in horror at the detail which had defeated them. Mary of Magdala, Mary the mother of the younger James and of Joses, Salome, the mother of Zebedee's sons, James and John, and some other women of Jesus' following watched and waited, hoping to understand.

Joseph recovered from the shock first. Since he had already planned to do so anyway, he went to Pilate and asked for Jesus' body. Joseph and Nicodemus then took the body off the cross. They and the women wrapped it in a shroud with spices and laid it in the nearby tomb Joseph had purchased. They had to hurry because the Sabbath, and the Passover, were about to begin. The men then went to John's house to process what had happened and to do what they could to rouse John from his depression. Eleazar was there, too, with the two Essenes expert in medicine and dressed in their traditional white robes. Their rescue mission had been aborted by the spear thrust.

Eleazar was serene. The monks were watchful and expectant. John was defeated, thoroughly defeated by an accident of life. "The jackals have won," he muttered. "We will never see the likes of him again on this planet. Is evil so strong we cannot successfully conspire against it, even in God's name?"

"That is probably the point," said Eleazar. "We cannot conspire against evil in God's name. Jesus gave himself up to evil. Whatever victory is forthcoming will be God's work, not ours. Wait and watch. We have learned that at Qumran: to wait and watch for God's victories."

Even Nicodemus, with all his brain power, still did not understand.

He lamented that they had come so close. It was as though when he had pulled the spikes out of Jesus' wrists that the nerve twitches had been those of reserved life, that not even the spear could take away.

John stood ramrod straight. To one of the monks he said, "The narcotic you prepared, it put Jesus in deep unconsciousness, did it not?"

The Essene nodded yes.

"His whole physical system would have been on hold when the spear thrust came," contributed Joseph. Then he too stood ramrod straight.

All three Jerusalem conspirators then headed for the door at the same time, three good men who desperately wanted to help God gain a victory that night. "There may still be life there!" exclaimed Nicodemus as he left the room. "It may not be too late!"

The Essenes followed respectfully as these dignified members of the highest council in Judaism ran toward the tomb of a dead man. It took all three of them to roll the heavy stone away from the entrance. Each had to stoop down to enter the small cave, and each was standing there transfixed when the monks arrived.

Jesus' body was gone. The shroud was there, but the body was gone. Eleazar motioned, and the two Essenes picked up either end of the shroud and took it out into the light of the Passover moon. The others slowly emerged from the cave, stunned and uncomprehending. The monks spread out the shroud and examined it closely. There was a faint image on it.

The light was not good, but there was little doubt it was the image of Jesus. The shroud was perfectly dry and appeared to be singed, but not by enough heat to destroy the cloth. It was as though the image had been formed in an instant burst of radiant energy in a millisecond of time.

In a few hours Mary of Magdala and the disciples discovered for themselves what God had done. The monks had gone back to try to interpret the agency of God to them at the tomb, but the hysteria of the moment rendered whatever they said inconsequential. Jesus had been raised from the dead.

On their way back to Qumran Eleazar and the Essenes talked about the current limitations of physics in describing the transfer of matter into energy. They talked about the creation itself and how it must have begun from pure energy in a flash of transmutation. They talked about the new creation they had just seen evidence of. They remembered how often Jesus had used the analogy of light to refer to God.

It appeared God had been involved in the planning of Jesus all along. "God was actually in Jesus," they thought. "Incredible."

"Do you think God was in Jesus from the beginning?" one of the Essenes asked Eleazar. "Or did Jesus assume God's blessing as he committed himself to the messiah's role and God's cause?"

It was a thoughtful question of the kind the old man had come to expect from these two. "Yes," he answered.

"Yes to which?"

"Yes to both and to many."

"I am convinced," continued Eleazar, "that some of us are born to God in a way we cannot escape.

But as we admit our parentage and are obedient, and as we try to think God's thoughts after him, God gives us special knowledge and power. That happened to Jesus after the Baptist's death. He became the Son of David, first in his mind, and later in reality. Simply put, Jesus planned and executed a brilliant campaign of conquest in God's name. We must give him credit for that, and for turning the idea of conquest inside out. Power will never be the same again. He was the messiah, but in a way many will never understand."

The monks understood. One of them said, "He was right about the ritual, too. It will help us remember."

"Not only that," said the other, "he could very well have founded a new religion.

Could you believe the activity level among those people back there? A lot of energy was being released."

Eleazar motioned for them to rest now by the side of the road to Qumran. He felt older today than usual. His sight was failing him, and he was as tired as the day was spent. Of course people would never believe this story the way it actually happened, but that did not matter very much. What they did believe would be close enough.

## AFTERWORD

*John the Priest came to understand these events in a profound way. We know his reflections upon them as* The Gospel According to John. *As an old man he wrote:*

*When all things began, the Word already was. The Word dwelt with God, and what God was, the Word was. The Word, then, was with God at the beginning, and through him all things came to be; no single thing was created without him. All that came to be was alive with his life, and that life was the light of men. The light shines on in the dark, and the darkness has never mastered it.*

*There appeared a man named John, sent from God; he came as a witness to testify to the light, that all might become believers through him. He was not himself the light; he came to bear witness to the light. The real light which enlightens every man was even then coming into the world.*

*He was in the world, but the world, though it owed its being to him, did not recognize him. He entered his own realm, and his own would not receive him. But to all who did receive him, to those who have yielded him their allegiance, he gave the right to become children of God, not born of any human stock, or by the fleshly desire of a human father, but the offspring of God himself. So the Word became flesh, he came to dwell among us, and we saw his glory, such glory as befits the Father's only Son, full of grace and truth.*

*Here is John's testimony to him: he cried aloud, 'This is the man I meant when I said, "He comes after me, but takes rank before me"; for before I was born, he already was.'*

*Out of his full store we have all received grace upon grace; for while the Law was given through Moses, grace and truth came through Jesus Christ. No one has ever seen God; but God's only Son, he who is nearest to the Father's heart, he has made him known.*

*The Christology of the 21st Century will know that once — some 18 billion years ago — matter was turned into energy in the primordial explosion we call the creation. Again, only two thousand years ago, another piece of matter was turned into energy in that singular event we call the resurrection. As new evidence mounts that the quasars are slowing down, that the universe is contracting, and that inevitably the result must be the black hole of complete matter reconstituted, it may also be remembered that once light not only comprehended the darkness, but that darkness cannot overcome it.*

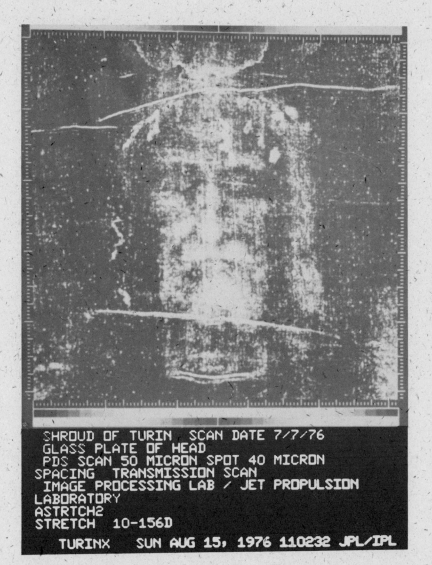

SHROUD OF TURIN   SCAN DATE 7/7/76
GLASS PLATE OF HEAD
PDS SCAN 50 MICRON SPOT 40 MICRON
SPACING   TRANSMISSION SCAN
IMAGE PROCESSING LAB / JET PROPULSION
LABORATORY
ASTRTCH2
STRETCH  10-156D

TURINX    SUN AUG 15, 1976 110232 JPL/IPL

*INDEX OF SYMBOLS*

## THE TREE OF JESSE

An angel told the Virgin Mary that Jesus would inherit "the throne of his father David" (Luke 1:32). King David's father was a seemingly innocuous man named Jesse, who lived in an old hut near Bethlehem. The designation of David as "the son of Jesse" was an opprobrious epithet used by those who hated Jesse's youngest son. The designation subsequently achieved a continuing venerability, however, while the expressions "shoot from the stump of Jesse" and "the root of Jesse" became pivotal symbols in messianic prophecy. The prophecy of Isaiah said, "And there shall come forth a shoot from the stump of Jesse, and a flower shall rise up out of his root....And the spirit of the Lord shall be the root of Jesse, who stands for an ensign of the people." (Isaiah 11:1,10)

The roots in this symbol are Jesse. The six-pointed star is the star of David. The plant and flower are Jesus. The chi rho are the first two letters of the Greek word for Christ and represent the kingship of the triumphant Christ.

## WISDOM

*The traditional symbol of wisdom is a burning lamp. Wisdom is presented in the Book of Proverbs as God's principal attribute. In the concept of the agency of God, it is his principal activity as well. In Proverbs 8:22-31, wisdom is personified as "the first-born of all creation," through whom "all things are made."*

*When Jesus sought wisdom, he did so in the particular context of the religion of ancient Israel, which held that wisdom functions within the lives of a covenanted people and eventually embraces sacral traditions. The sacral traditions choose to identify human good with divine intention.*

*Wisdom said that man's welfare is its goal, and prudence its manner of acting. Such pragmatism arose from a religious conviction about the order of the universe. Right behavior constitutes life itself; hence, it transcends mere moral obligation. Every proverb or artifact of human experience arises within history, and the totality of the wisdom literature which Jesus mastered created a unique history of its own, both linguistic and ideological. Jesus thoroughly subscribed to the longstanding conviction of his people that wisdom is historical and that God can only be known in historical events.*

## THE CROSS AND CROWN

*The developed understanding of the Son of David, the messiah, as a suffering servant and not as a triumphant warrior and political leader was a quantum leap in the religious thought of ancient Israel. The idea's appropriation by Jesus was the work of a religious genius who was very much aware of the tradition he chose to embody and live out. A strong element in this tradition was a prayer recited regularly at synagogue worship and adapted from Isaiah 11 and Psalm 132: "Speedily cause the branch of David, thy servant, to sprout, and let his horn be exalted by thy salvation; because daily do we wait for thy salvation."*

*The symbol of cross and crown claims kingship after all for the branch of David who became an offering for sin and thereby the instrument of salvation. The cross signifies that suffering was indeed the route to this kingship and that the sacrifice of the Son of David brought atonement, at-one-ment, to the people of both the old and the new Israel, the Church. The crossed palm branches are a symbol of victory and are reminiscent of the practice of Judaism in using palm branches, boughs of leafy trees, and willows in observing the Feast of Tabernacles. "You shall take choice fruits, palm branches, boughs of leafy trees, and willows from the river bank, and for seven days you shall rejoice in the presence of Yahweh your God." (Leviticus 23:40)*

## THE DESCENDING DOVE

*The descending dove is one of the most familiar representations of the Holy Spirit. Biblical reference to this symbol is found in the baptism of Jesus. "As soon as Jesus was baptized he came up from the water, and suddenly the heavens opened up for him and he saw the spirit of God descending like a dove and coming down on him. And a voice spoke from heaven, 'This is my son, the beloved; my favor rests on him'."*
*(Matthew 3:16-17)*

*In the theology of the early church the spirit which hovered over the waters at the first creation (Genesis 1:2) reappeared at the beginning of the new creation, the baptism of Jesus. The spirit had two functions: it anointed Jesus for his messianic mission which the spirit was to guide, and it sanctified God's old enemy, the waters, thus preparing the way for Christian baptism. The primordial waters in Genesis had signified chaos, out of which God made order. Now the waters signified regeneration, a new order, and a restatement of the covenant between God and man.*

*The dove is white and has a three-rayed nimbus, a symbol of the trinity. The nimbus distinguishes the image from the dove of peace, a symbol used by numerous non-Christian groups.*

## THE SCEPTER

*The scepter is a symbol of royal authority, especially emblematic of the king's striking power. In the ancient world it was a stylized descendent of the shepherd's staff, the farmer's flail, and a weapon wielded by warriors. In the Roman hegemony the rod of the scepter was topped with the head of an eagle.*

*A scepter is almost invariably a feature of Near Eastern royal portraits, and was undoubtedly part of the Israelite kings' royal regalia. In the Old Testament, the scepter of Yahweh, the supreme king, was said to be the tribe of Judah, to which the Davidic monarch belonged. Thus the Davidic kingship was an extension of the divine authority.*

*Messianism adopted the metaphor of the scepter in Numbers 24:17: "A scepter shall rise out of Israel," and in Ezekiel 19 the prophetic vision was that the vine, Israel, would grow tall and its strongest branch would become the ruler's scepter. Elsewhere the scepter was the instrument of God's justice: "Your throne, God, shall last for ever and ever, your royal scepter is a scepter of integrity." (Psalm 45:6) "From his mouth came a sharp sword to strike the pagans with; he is the one who will rule them with an iron scepter, and tread out the wine of Almighty God's fierce anger. On his cloak and on his standard there was a name written: the King of kings and the Lord of lords." (Revelation 19:15-16)*

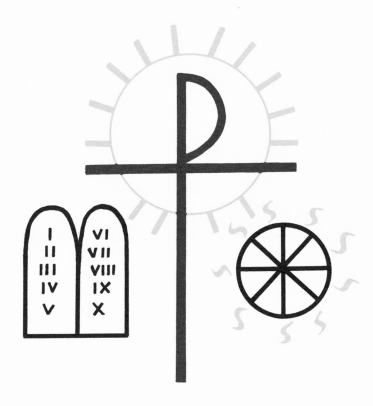

## THE TRANSFIGURATION

*The first three gospels (Matthew 17:1-8; Mark 9:2-8; Luke 9:28-36) record an event in which Jesus took three chosen disciples to a mountaintop to pray. As Peter, James, and John watched, Jesus' face became radiant, and Moses and Elijah seemed to be talking with him. Peter wanted to put up three tentlike shelters (tabernacles or booths) for them. The disciples were overcome with awe and said they heard a voice coming out of a cloud: "This is my beloved son; listen to him." (Mark 9:7)*

*Moses represented the law given earlier on another mountain, Sinai, hence the tablets in the symbol. Elijah represented Israel's prophets, hence the burning wheel of the chariot of fire which had borne Elijah to heaven. Moses and Elijah had come to do homage to the founder of the new alliance between God and man.*

*The radiant <u>chi rho</u> in the center of the symbol is a sacred monogram formed from the first two letters of the Greek word for Christ. These letters took the English letters X and P, although the X was frequently simplified to a cross bar (†) on the walls of the catacombs, as well as on pottery, coins, sarcophagi, and other artifacts of the early church.*

## PASSOVER

*The Passover is a spring festival in Judaism which commemorates the deliverance of the Hebrew people from slavery in Egypt. The blood of the lamb killed for the original Passover was put on the lintels and posts of the doors of houses where the people of Israel dwelled, hence the symbol. The blood served as a signal to the "destroyer" to <u>pass over</u> these houses on his mission to slay the first-born of the Egyptians. The full story is recounted in the Book of Exodus, Chapter 12.*

*In subsequent generations a ritually slain lamb — a "paschal" lamb from the Hebrew word for Passover, <u>pasah</u> — was dressed with legs unbroken and became the basis for a solemn banquet. During the meal a designated "son" of the family asked the ceremonial question, "Why is this night different from all other nights?" This introduced the recital in song and story of God's acts of redemption throughout Israel's long history. Over the years the Passover thus became Israel's festival of freedom. Its sacramental implications were appropriated by Jesus as he turned the Passover meal into the Last Supper on the night of his arrest and trial. In Christian theology Jesus became the paschal lamb who was slain as a sacrifice, and who brought deliverance to the captives of sin.*

## GRAPES AND WHEAT

Bunches of grapes and spikes of wheat form the symbol of the sacrament of the Last Supper. Flour made from wheat is the usual ingredient of bread, about which Jesus said at the Last Supper, "This is my body, which is for you...." The grapes, like the wine of Communion, represent the blood of Jesus, following his words, "This cup is the new covenant sealed in my blood."

On other occasions Jesus said such things as, "I am the bread of life. He who comes to me will never be hungry," and "I am the vine, you are the branches. Cut off from me you can do nothing."

The elements of the Last Supper were called "supernatural food" in the epistles of the New Testament. They were compared to the Old Testament manna and water from the rock enjoyed by the Hebrews wandering through the wilderness to the Promised Land. (I Corinthians 10) The sacrament came to share many of the motifs of the Jewish Passover, primarily that of communal remembrance. Today it is a thankful and joyous memorial of redemption, understood not only as a mental recollection of past events, but as a contemporary experience of the mighty deliverance of God. The Eucharist derived from the Last Supper is central to the act of worship in the Roman Catholic Church.

## THE CROSS

The cross is the most familiar symbol of Christianity. Protestants usually use the empty cross, especially on the altar, to emphasize the risen and victorious Christ. Scholars have estimated that there are over four hundred forms of the cross, with approximately fifty of these used in Christian symbolism. This design is called the Latin cross, which has the upper arm and the two sides of equal length and the lower arm twice as long.

Roman soldiers used many forms of crucifixion. Typically the cross was a stake sunk vertically in the ground with the victim suspended on it with spikes about five inches long. Often, but not always, a horizontal piece was attached to the vertical stake, sometimes at the top to give the shape of a T, and sometimes just below the top, producing the form most familiar in Christian symbolism. The cross was Rome's most ignominious form of execution.

As the victim's body sagged on the cross, gradually his body was asphyxiated. Recent archaeological evidence from a victim found in a first century A.D. tomb in Jerusalem, with a spike still piercing his heel bones, indicates the spikes on the horizontal piece of the cross were nailed into the victim's forearms between the radius and the ulna.

INRI

# INRI

INRI is a sacred monogram abbreviating the Latin words "*Jesus Nazarene Rex Iudaeorum,*" meaning "Jesus of Nazareth, King of the Jews." (Latin does not use the letter "J".) This is the inscription the Roman governor, Pontius Pilate, ordered to be placed over the cross of Jesus. (John 19:19)

Pilate ordered the inscription as his commentary on what he considered the unjust charge of political intrigue brought against Jesus by his enemies in the highest council of Judaism, the Sanhedrin. Pilate refused to change the wording of the inscription to, "*He said I am* King of the Jews."

Thus the irony stands. Jesus was what his enemies said he was, what Pilate said he was, and what the Davidic succession said he was in his role as messiah.

## THE LAMB OF GOD

*The paschal lamb was the lamb without blemish slain and eaten by faithful Jews at Passover. (Exodus 12:1-13) Jesus died at Passover, and is often called in Christian theology the paschal lamb or paschal victim.*

*The interpretation of Jesus as the Lamb of God first occurred in John 1:29, where John the Baptist said of Jesus, "Behold, the Lamb of God (in Latin, Ecce Agnus Dei) who takes away the sin of the world."*

*In this symbol the standing lamb bearing the cross-emblazoned banner of victory signifies the resurrection. Representing Jesus as the Son of God, the lamb has a three-rayed nimbus to designate a member of the trinity. The banner is a swallow-tailed pennon.*

*An Easter hymn originally in the Latin Breviary emphasized the origin of this symbol in the tradition of the paschal lamb. The hymn is entitled, "At the Lamb's High Feast We Sing," and closes with:*

*"Now thy banner thou dost wave;*
*Vanquished Satan and the grave."*

## THE CROSS AND SHROUD

*A shroud is a cloth in which a corpse is wrapped for burial. The symbol of the cross and shroud represents the period beginning with the removal of Jesus' body from the cross by Joseph of Arimathea and Nicodemus (John 18:38-40), and ending with the resurrection. The first evidence of the resurrection was "the linen cloth lying there" by itself in the tomb. (John 20:5)*

*The Shroud of Turin is believed by many to be the actual burial cloth of Jesus. It is a piece of linen 14 feet 3 inches long by 3 feet 7 inches wide, and rests in the Cathedral of St. John the Baptist in Turin, Italy. Microbiologists have established that pollens indigenous to the area around Jerusalem are still in the shroud, and hematologists have demonstrated that the blood markings identified by forensic pathologists are in fact human blood. The clump of thorns which pierced the scalp of the victim depicted on the shroud was a form of punishment reserved specifically for Jesus of Nazareth. Two of the spikes which pierced the body are shown on the shroud as having pierced the wrists, not the hands, a fact unknown to medieval artists and forgers.*

## THE SUN AND CHI RHO

*An honored description of the messiah is in the last chapter of the Old Testament: "The sun of righteousness shall rise, with healing in its wings." (Malachi 4:2) The sun is the source of light. In Christian thought Jesus is referred to frequently as the light: "All that came to be was alive with his life, and that life was the light of men." (John 1:4)*

*The sun of righteousness became a title used by Christians for Jesus. The chi rho in the middle of the winged sun is a familiar monogram formed from the first two letters of the Greek word for Christ. The symbol of the sun and chi rho is based on the widespread representation in the ancient Near East of the solar diety as a winged disc.*

*In Hebrew cosmogony and eschatology the sun was fashioned and placed in the firmament on the fourth day of creation, to light the earth during the day and to regulate the seasons. Prophecy says that when all things revert to primordial chaos, the sun will be darkened or will stand still. At the final triumph of Yahweh, however, a new order will be created and the winged sun will shine sevenfold as bright as it ever shined on the brightest day. (Isaiah 30:26)*

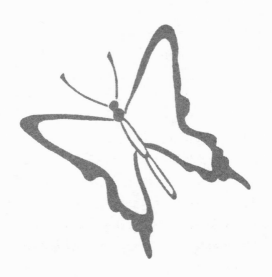

## THE BUTTERFLY

This insect is a symbol of Jesus' resurrection. The caterpillar goes into a cocoon, understood in early Christian theology as a larval tomb, where it seemingly dies, only to emerge as a beautiful butterfly. More specifically, the chrysalis stage of the pupa corresponds to the body of Jesus in the grave. The pupa bursting the outer covering and emerging as a butterfly signifies Christ's victory over death and the grave. Since Christ's victory is also the believer's victory, the symbol represents the resurrection of the body for all Christians.

"Larva" is defined in Webster's Seventh New Collegiate Dictionary as, "the early form of any animal that at birth or hatching is fundamentally unlike its parent and must metamorphose before assuming adult characteristics."

## THE SHIP

*The ship is one of the earliest symbols for the church. It is designed with a cross-shaped mast and is shown sailing through troubled waters. The church, like a ship, carries the faithful through all conditions of life.*

*The symbolism recalls the story of Jesus calming the storm on the Sea of Galilee. (Matthew 8:23-27; Mark 4:35-41; Luke 8:22-25) Matthew says, "Without warning a storm broke over the sea, so violent that the waves were breaking over the boat." The disciples implored Jesus, "Save us, Lord, we are going down!" Jesus then rebuked the wind and said to the sea, "Quiet now! Be calm!" And, Mark says, "The wind dropped and all was calm again." All three synoptic gospel writers record the disciples' response. Luke says, "They were awestruck and astonished and said to one another 'Who can this be, that gives orders even to winds and waves and they obey him?'"*

*From the Latin word for ship comes the term "nave" to designate the central part of the interior of a church building. The similar word "navel" marks the central point of attachment for the cord which sustains the life of a human being in the womb.*

## THE CANDLE

*Although candles were not used in biblical times, the Hebrew and Greek words for lamp were translated into candle in the King James Version of the Bible (1611) and entered the Christian lexicon as the symbol for light, warmth, and devotion.*

*The candle or oil-based lamp is a localization of light, which universally symbolized life in biblical times. This accounts for the widespread practice of placing lamps in tombs, the realm of darkness. Light stands for the divine presence (Revelation 21:23; 22:5; John 8:12; I John 1:5; etc.), and consequently for those things emanating from or related to the divine presence. The prophetic word was said to be a lamp shining in the darkness. (John 5:35; II Peter 1:19; Mark 4:21-22; Luke 8:16-17) The lamp was also seen as a transforming light representing the law (Psalm 119:105; Proverbs 6:23) or works of righteousness. (Matthew 5:15) The lamp is a symbol of the lasting existence of the Davidic dynasty in I Kings 11:36; 15:4; II Kings 8:18; and II Chronicles 21:7. God himself is the lamp lighting the darkness in II Samuel 22:29. The root of this pervasive symbol in scripture is in the light-life equation, although wisdom also says life is not the wick or the candle. It is the burning.*

## THE FISH

*The fish is an ancient symbol for Christ as savior. It appears in the art of the oldest Christian catacombs as a cipher. The Greek word for fish, ICHTHYS, has five letters, the initials of which mean "Jesus Christ, Son of God, Savior."*

*The symbol of the fish was an identification device for early Christians under persecution, since it was easy to draw. Later it became a talisman for bishops and popes portrayed as fishers of men. In the writings of the apostolic fathers' believers were sometimes described as fish caught from the sea of sin through baptism.*

## HEAD OF CHRIST

*This is the first of a series of eight heads of Christ painted by the Dutch master, Rembrandt van Rijn (1606-1669). It is oil on a panel 8 x 9¾ inches and hangs in the painting gallery of the State Museum in Berlin.*

*The significance of this painting is that earlier artists had almost always depicted Jesus with idealized features in accord with their period's conception of his divine nature. Rembrandt's Jesus was based on his study of serious-minded young Jews living around him, and on his study of the scriptural passages which reveal aspects of Jesus' personality and character. For this portrait Rembrandt was particularly influenced by Hebrews 2:16-17: "He took not on him the nature of angels, but he took on him the seed of Abraham, wherefore in all things he considered it well to be like his brethren."*

## SAINT JOHN THE EVANGELIST

The word "evangelist" means one who proclaims good tidings. In the New Testament an evangelist was one who traveled from place to place preaching the gospel. The authors of the four gospels were referred to in the early centuries of the Christian Church as The Four Evangelists, and tradition designated a symbol for each. Each evangelist was a creature with wings: Matthew was a winged man, because he began his gospel by describing the human lineage of Jesus; Mark was a winged lion, because he began his gospel by describing John the Baptist crying in the wilderness as a lion of Judah; Luke was a winged ox, because his gospel vividly described the sacrificial death of Jesus; John was an eagle, because it was said his gospel "soared on eagle's wings" and emphasized the ascension.

The Gospel of John was probably written near the end of the first century, at least 60 years after the death of Jesus. It was written well after the synoptic gospels of Matthew, Mark, and Luke, and represents a theological perspective distinct from them. The uniqueness of the Fourth Gospel caused some hesitancy in the early church to accept it as authoritative and canonical, although its account of the last days of Jesus' life is generally considered more accurate than that of the synoptics. Saint John the Evangelist was a primary source for the The Son of David.

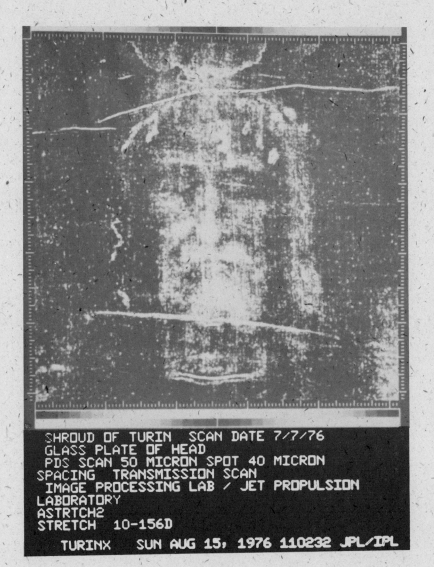

SHROUD OF TURIN   SCAN DATE 7/7/76
GLASS PLATE OF HEAD
PDS SCAN 50 MICRON SPOT 40 MICRON
SPACING  TRANSMISSION SCAN
 IMAGE PROCESSING LAB / JET PROPULSION
LABORATORY
ASTRTCH2
STRETCH  10-156D

    TURINX    SUN AUG 15, 1976 110232 JPL/IPL

## IMAGE ON THE SHROUD OF TURIN

*Some scholars believe this is a photograph of Jesus in death. The full-body image on the shroud is that of a crucified adult male between thirty and thirty-five years of age with a body weight of approximately 175 pounds and a height of about five feet, ten inches. The image is best seen and studied as a photographic negative, which means light and dark on the image are reversed.*

*Light and dark are also distance-coded, which means the image is three-dimensional. It is entirely a surface phenomenon, however, existing only on the top one-thousandth of the shroud's linen fibers. Computer analysis shows the image to be completely random in its constituency, indicating it has no directional brush marks and could not have been painted. Scientific research has proved beyond any reasonable doubt that the image on the Shroud of Turin is not a forgery. It was probably formed by a sudden burst of radiation as the body it once represented was changed from matter into energy.*